Praise for *Fulton J. Sheen*

"Alexis Walkenstein offers us more than just a glimpse into the life and ministry of Bishop Fulton Sheen. She provides us an opportunity to continue to be inspired by his beautiful teachings and to walk with him on our journey of faith. It is that gift of faith and love of Christ that has guided Alexis in her selection of Bishop Sheen's writings. This book can be our companion as we reflect on the joy of Christ in our lives."

—Séan Cardinal O'Malley, OFM, Cap.,
Archbishop of Boston

"Don't know much about Fulton Sheen? Me either!
"Too busy to sit down and read one of his books? Me too!
"Alexis has given us the best of both worlds: Bishop Sheen for those with spiritual ADD . . ."

—Lino Rulli, *The Catholic Guy*,
SiriusXM Satellite Radio

"[This book is] an essential compendium of the Venerable Archbishop's writings, revealing the heart of his sanctity. They joyfully inspire us to realize that, in the words of his renowned television series, *life is worth living*."

—Most Reverend Gerald M. Barbarito,
Bishop of Palm Beach

"Accept Alexis Walkenstein's compelling invitation to become a spiritual student of Venerable Fulton J. Sheen, and find your life transformed!"

—Lisa M. Hendey,
author of *The Grace of Yes*

"For years I have been inspired by the Venerable Bishop Sheen; now I feel as if he's an old friend in these pearls from his library of wisdom."

—Most Reverend Robert P. Reed,
Auxiliary Bishop of Boston,
President and CEO of iCatholic Media

"Walkenstein's powerful introduction sets the stage for this compilation of Sheen's practical wisdom. A great read for the busy soul in search of meaning today!"

—Fr. Daniel Hennessey,
Director of Vocations, Archdiocese of Boston

"Alexis Walkenstein provides the reader with perfectly selected excerpts of some of the Bishop's most inspiring books. His beautiful words are truly those of a Saint!"

—Rosemarie Holliger Costello, Archbishop Fulton J. Sheen Foundation Advisory Council, relative of the late Archbishop Fulton J. Sheen

"One of the biggest mistakes we can make as twenty-first-century disciples of Christ is to ignore the wisdom of Fulton J. Sheen, assuming that his advice is dated and not applicable to today's world. In this compilation of his writings, Alexis Walkenstein helps us discover that Sheen's wisdom is every bit as pertinent today as when it was first written. Highly recommended!"

—Gary Zimak, speaker, author,
radio host, www.followingthetruth.com

"Possibly no soul in the past century has had a greater impact on the Church in America than Archbishop Fulton Sheen did. A man of incredible intellect and undeniable charisma, Sheen's words, wit, and wisdom are on full display in *Ex Libris: Fulton J. Sheen*. What a gift Walkenstein has given to the Church in this compilation. Not only will those souls blessed to remember this great man of God now have quick access to some of his finest theological gems, but an entirely new generation—my own kids—will be immeasurably blessed by this future saint's glory-filled perspective. Offering insights and snippets on everything from prayer to sex, and marriage to mercy, some of Fulton's Sheen's best explanations and challenges allow even the novice reader to avail themselves of timeless wisdom for modern times. As a life-long fan of Fulton Sheen, I can think of no greater gift than a book like this ... allowing my own kids and an entirely new generation of young Catholics to learn about the Master from a master."

—Mark Hart, Executive Vice President, Life Teen International;
co-host, *The Catholic Guy*, SiriusXM Satellite Radio;
best-selling Catholic author and speaker

"Bishop Sheen's timeless insights and advice have never been more needed. But he wrote so many volumes, it's hard to know where to begin. Alexis Walkenstein has solved this problem. This is like a chocolate sampler of Sheen's wisdom. Prepare to be surprised, transformed, and initiated into the mind and heart of Fulton Sheen."

—Raymond Arroyo,
New York Times best-selling author, broadcaster

Fulton J. Sheen

Ex Libris

Fulton J. Sheen

Compiled by Alexis Walkenstein

Pauline
BOOKS & MEDIA

Library of Congress Cataloging-in-Publication Data

Names: Sheen, Fulton J. (Fulton John), 1895-1979, author. | Walkenstein, Alexis, editor.

Title: Fulton J. Sheen / compiled by Alexis Walkenstein.

Description: Boston, MA : Pauline Books & Media, 2018. | Series: Ex Libris series | Includes bibliographical references.

Identifiers: LCCN 2017038754| ISBN 9780819827470 (pbk.) | ISBN 0819827479 (pbk.)

Subjects: LCSH: Spiritual life--Catholic Church.

Classification: LCC BX2350.3 .S535 2018 | DDC 282--dc23

LC record available at https://lccn.loc.gov/2017038754

Copyright permission was granted by The Estate of Fulton J. Sheen/The Society for the Propagation of the Faith/www.mission.org

The Scripture quotations contained herein are directly quoted from works written by Fulton J. Sheen.

Cover design by Rosana Usselmann

Cover photo Bettmann/Getty Images

Published by Pauline Books & Media, 50 Saint Pauls Avenue, Boston, MA 02130-3491

Printed in the U.S.A.

www.pauline.org

Pauline Books & Media is the publishing house of the Daughters of St. Paul, an international congregation of women religious serving the Church with the communications media.

1 2 3 4 5 6 7 8 9   22 21 20 19 18

For my future husband.

Contents

✦⊶ DIVINE LOVE ⊷✦

✦⊶ SIN ⊷✦

✦⊶ KNOWING JESUS ⊷✦

Introduction

I call him *my* saint. I also call him my hero, my "New York minute" maneuverer, my bishop in heaven, and my communications master.

But for a long time, all I really knew about Fulton J. Sheen was that he was a famous TV bishop of my parents' generation. In the '50s and '60s, people from all backgrounds—Jews, Christians, and non-believers—gathered around the television on Sunday evenings for Bishop Sheen's popular broadcasts. When they were children, both my then-Jewish dad in Revere, Massachusetts, and my Catholic mother in suburban Natick, Massachusetts, would gather with family around their TV sets to watch Bishop Sheen's TV shows *Life Is Worth Living* and later *The Fulton Sheen Program*. Sheen's charismatic preaching style was joyful, fervent, full of common sense, and at times even hauntingly prophetic. Everyone wanted to watch the bishop with the chalkboard, piercing eyes, and disarming wit.

I began to know Fulton Sheen around the time I was offered a position as communications director for a diocese in south Florida. When I accepted the job, I knew I was walking into a difficult situation. I would be assisting a new bishop who was assigned to renew and reform a diocese that was still reeling from the sex abuse scandals. I was a faithful Catholic and had covered the Church as a mainstream journalist, but I didn't really know what it would be like to work for a bishop or the Church.

Before I embarked on my 1,400-mile drive from Boston to Florida, I wandered into a local Catholic bookstore and perused the shelves, hoping to find a spiritual work to mark my move and inspire my next assignment. Almost immediately, I plucked *Three to Get Married* by Fulton Sheen from the shelves. Intrigued by the book's topic, I wondered if this holy bishop could help me on two fronts: my newly appointed service to a bishop and the Church as well as my desire for marriage.

After I bought the book, I tossed it into my trunk amid suitcases, boxes, and all my life's possessions. It was soon forgotten, buried in the back of my petite convertible for the unforeseen future. *Three to Get Married* didn't surface until I was getting ready to sell my car and was cleaning out the trunk a few years after I arrived in Florida. When I saw the book, it was as though it became illuminated, drawing me to it. I heard God say in my heart, *"You can't just have a vocation to marriage and not prepare."*

I read Sheen's book several times and it moved me deeply. Not just because of the topic, but also because Sheen was a teacher who imparted wisdom relevant to every human person striving for meaning in his or her life. He presented the power of the Sacrament of Marriage with great pastoral care and seriousness. His Catholic approach to marriage clashed with the frivolity of our contemporary event-centric culture. But I appreciated that Sheen didn't mince words. Faith comes from hearing the word of God, and Sheen knew who he was as a bishop: a teacher. He fully lived his episcopal office to teach and instruct.

As I read the book, I felt inspired to ask Sheen to intercede for me amid the difficult challenges I was facing at my job. The diocese where I worked was still in ongoing repair after the sex abuse scandals and was currently dealing with a serious financial embezzlement scandal. I instinctively felt that Sheen was the perfect intercessor for me at this moment in my life and for the situation of the diocese I worked in at the time.

I began to read Sheen's many books and watch his television shows. I learned that he taught not just with his provocative and impactful words on the airwaves and in books, but in every way he lived his priestly life. He lived a charism of being present to people. He didn't remain locked behind the closed doors of a rectory; he spent himself for the Church. He was out with people, serving the laity and taking time for the poor. The presence of Christ in Sheen was not restrained but rather shared—poured out so that all who encountered him might encounter Jesus through his episcopal office.

Sheen's charisma and holy way of life intrigued me, but there was also a personal connection. He was an Emmy-award winning TV bishop, and I had won an Emmy during my local television news days when I worked in New York. In a way, I had been grieving leaving my secular career, but here was this Emmy-toting bishop modeling for me how to bridge both the world of media and the Church. His witness spilled out of traditional Church forums and permeated popular culture. As a bishop, he used his platform to reach millions.

When I worked in mainstream television news, I had seen the power of the platform to do good and inspire even amid the tragic and difficult stories that make up so much of secular news. As a journalist, I felt guided by the Holy Spirit to tell stories of incredible human triumph, witness, and resilience. As God led me from mainstream television news toward more direct evangelization in the Church, I felt called to bring the Gospel to the world through media in a new, bolder way. Sheen was a model for me of this kind of evangelization. He was also an intercessor as I made this step in my personal witness and expression of the faith.

Clearly, Sheen was my God-sent heavenly reinforcement, a bishop-intercessor not only for me but also for my diocese and the Church. Sheen was a bishop who was unafraid to lead the Church in season and out of season, just the intercessor needed for the newly assigned bishop of my diocese. Sheen is not yet a saint, and I did not know that much about him. But I did know that Sheen was a reformer, and my diocese needed renewal. Sheen was also a master of communications media, and I was working with the media every day. Like Sheen, I strove to teach when I interacted with the press, not just with a mere "no comment" or defensive statements, but with authentic evangelization. I shared positive stories of hope with the religious press, but also with the mainstream media. Sheen was an intercessor and a model for such a time as this.

A few years ago in December, the women in my family took a mini road trip to New York City for a "girls' weekend," which included holiday shows, shopping, and some unexpected signs from my new holy friend. Of course, you can't visit New York without stopping at St. Patrick's Cathedral. So, we made a visit to the cathedral and a few of us stayed behind to take in the beauty, go to Mass, and spend time in prayer. At one point, I saw my mom and my Aunt Suzanne kneeling behind the main altar, so I knelt down next to them to unite our prayers as a family. As I knelt, I read the engraved plaque on my kneeler. It was in honor of "Servant of God Fulton J. Sheen" and included a prayer to advance his cause for canonization. I had been asking for Sheen's intercession, but I had not known that he was on his way to becoming a saint!

My spiritual friendship with Sheen had culminated in this huge grace-filled realization that my new bishop friend was already on his way to becoming a saint. This was a strong confirmation that he was truly helping me—in my work, in my sacrifice of a successful secular career, in my waiting and preparing for a God-sent husband, in my sufferings and joys, and in my family life.

I became lost in the moment, keenly aware that while we sometimes choose the saints we like and are attracted to, at other times *they* choose us. The reality of the saints is that *they are as alive as we are.* This is particularly true in the case of Fulton Sheen, a bishop whose love for life was accompanied by a joy and humor that were contagious. I marveled that there are no coincidences with God. It was as if time stood still in that moment.

Suddenly, it occurred to me that Bishop Sheen was probably buried in the crypt below the main altar. Unabashedly, I summoned the security guard and asked if Sheen was "down there." With a typical New York-style eye roll, he responded, "Yeah." Determined, I pressed on and petitioned to be allowed down below. Reluctantly the guard said, "Hang on, let me get the sacristan." As we waited on our respective kneelers for permission to enter the crypt, I was bursting inside, knowing we were just a few steps away from the saint-to-be.

The security guard finally returned with an older sacristan who had more keys hanging from his neck than a garage attendant. The sacristan told us that he could bring us down to the crypt after the next Mass. We told him we'd wait. After the Mass, he brought my mom, my aunt, and me beneath the main altar into the crypt, which housed many of New York's successors to the Apostles—bishops, cardinals, and now Fulton J. Sheen. We knelt on the cement floor and pressed our bodies as close as we could to Sheen's resting place. I asked Sheen to pray for five seemingly impossible situations. I offered him my heart and my intentions, and silently ended by saying, "and I will promote you if you help me."

Promote him.

I didn't really know what that last part of my prayer meant. It wasn't something that I would ordinarily say. I was certainly not bargaining with God; the prayer just welled up inside me. Looking back, I believe I was recognizing a call from God to help others to know this holy TV bishop in heaven. That he responds to prayers. That the truth he lived is Jesus' truth, and that with his help we can understand Jesus and the Church better and be led on the path of a life truly worth living. After what seemed like an eternity, we emerged from the crypt and I suddenly burst out laughing. It occurred to me that promoting Sheen was a win-win situation. He's already famous!

Little did I know that I was about to get my first assignment from this "New York minute" bishop. . . .

As my family and I walked down Fifth Avenue away from St. Patrick's Cathedral, I turned on my phone and checked my email. At the top of my inbox was an email from a priest I had never met before, Father Stanley Deptula, the executive director of the Fulton J. Sheen Foundation in Peoria, Illinois. He was reaching out to ask if I would help him "promote Bishop Sheen in South Florida." MIC DROP.

I immediately raised the phone high to the heavens and declared, "My prayers are being answered!" I shoved my phone in my family's astonished faces and then executed a flurry of email exchanges with now-Monsignor Deptula. I excitedly explained that, just minutes before, I had prayed to Fulton J. Sheen inside the crypt of St. Patrick's Cathedral. He said he wasn't surprised and that this was typically how Sheen operated. He asked if my diocese would be interested in supporting the cause for the canonization of then-Servant of God Fulton J. Sheen. YES.

With my bishop's generous permission, I helped to organize a series of events in my diocese. We reintroduced Sheen to those who already knew and loved him and brought him to an entirely new generation, including young families and seminarians. God was hearing my prayer and was touching both the diocese and the Church that I loved. This work of evangelization became a real labor of love for me. I felt like the veil between heaven and earth was very thin in this grace-filled time. I was keenly aware that as I promoted Sheen's cause alongside my day-to-day work in the Church, God would be busy on my behalf.

In the midst of our work to promote Bishop Sheen, another surprise occurred. An elderly woman in the diocese who was a friend of Bishop Sheen heard about the local events and introduced me to Bishop Sheen's niece, Joan Sheen Cunningham. When I found out about Joan, I invited her to attend the Masses that would be offered in honor of her late uncle to promote his cause for sainthood.

Joan's presence in our diocese and witness to her uncle's life of virtue and holiness were extraordinary blessings. Fulton Sheen was not only an uncle but a spiritual father to Joan, who had often accompanied him as a young girl. She revealed to me certain aspects of her uncle's holy way of life, some not widely known. For instance, Joan told me that Sheen never drank alcohol. She shared with me how joyful and playful he was when interacting with people, the urgency he felt for souls, and his "love for love" as he played match-maker for couples. She told me that he spent time in prayer with Jesus in a eucharistic Holy Hour every day. He was also very generous; he often gave his coat away, right off his back, when he encountered someone in need. Joan also told me how he had a heart for the missions his entire life, and often ministered to his brother priests.

When you read the lives of the saints, they often have a pack of saintly people who accompanied them in life. Now I was sitting, conversing, and relating with one of Sheen's "posse." Joan made me feel personally welcomed into Bishop Sheen's family, and she extended that same hospitality to those who turned out for the events in honor of her uncle. After dropping her off at her hotel one evening, I wept as I drove home. In meeting Joan, I felt as if I had met a part of Fulton Sheen. I felt closer to him then more than ever before. As I drove, I prayed that many people would get to know Christ more through Sheen's spirituality and his holy example. I would later meet many more of Sheen's relatives and friends, and each impacted me deeply. Soon I was surrounded by Sheen's "posse"—and I was their newest member!

Fulton Sheen lived his life to the full and for the glory of God because *he knew God*. He knew the person of Jesus Christ and he knew who *he* was as a son of God, especially as a priest. That zeal propelled Bishop Sheen to spread the Catholic faith to saints and sinners alike, so that everyone could come to know their identity in Jesus Christ. Sheen's zeal urged him to evangelize not just on TV, but also in hospitals, on airplanes, in the streets, in his family, with the Hollywood elite, as a media pioneer, with strangers, with the homeless and the unwanted—in America and all over the world. Sheen taught in word and deed how to know, love, and serve God, which is the fundamental reason for our existence. This call to know, love, and serve God remains relevant and even more urgent today.

Bishop Sheen called people out. Out of sin and into new life. Out of bad habits and self-centeredness and into relationship with God and service to one another. Ever since my initial encounter with saint-to-be Fulton J. Sheen, I have wanted to shout from the rooftops the very many things God has done through Sheen's intercession. I want to lead others to learn what I have learned from his powerful teaching. Bishop Sheen is the special saint-to-be for a new generation.

This book is your personal invitation to be renewed in Christ, in the school of Fulton Sheen. In the pages that follow, you will encounter the wisdom of this spiritual powerhouse in words of encouragement and challenge—for the faithful as well as for seekers. Whether you picked up this book yourself or someone else picked it up for you, there are no coincidences with God. I became Fulton Sheen's "spiritual student" without realizing at first what was happening. There is a reason that *you* too are here now with Bishop Sheen.

Over the years, Fulton Sheen produced a lot of content to choose from, but in this book I focus on five main areas of his thought: the mystery of God, freedom, God's love, sin, and Jesus. As you sit at the feet of this great teacher, contemplate the inescapable love of God for you personally and how he is calling you through Sheen's words. While reading, try to surrender your will to God's divine will, and embrace your vocation of love in imitation of Christ's great love for you.

God can transform your life through the redemptive power present in the Gospel that Sheen preached. I hope you accept his invitation to be set apart, set free, and set on fire for a life in Christ—a life worth living because Jesus lives in you.

—Alexis Walkenstein

JMJ+

GOD IS FIRE

*Because God is Fire, we cannot escape Him, whether
we draw near for conversion or flee from aversion: In
either case He affects us. If we accept His love, its fires
will illumine and warm us; if we reject Him, they
will still burn on in us in frustration and remorse.*

—Peace of Soul, 242

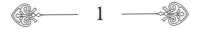

The Soul and God

God solicits each of us by a dialogue no other soul can hear. His action on the soul is always for us alone. He sends no circular letters, uses no party lines.[1] God never deals with crowds as crowds—they could give Him only earthly glory—but what He wants is each soul's singular and secret fealty. He calls His sheep by name; He leaves the ninety-nine that are safe to find the one that is lost. On the Cross He addresses the thief in the second person singular: "This day, *thou* shalt be with Me in Paradise."[2] God never sells His bread of life wholesale. He tempers the wind to the individual sheep; He heals the particular man. Once the soul becomes conscious of the Divine Presence, it feels itself under a Divine Imperative and whispers to itself: "This is a message sent to me and no one else." This inner influence of God, which is so personal, arouses it to a knowledge of its own responsibility—we know, now, that it was God Whom we offended in the past. External things are no longer blamed for the soul's condition; rather, we strike our breast and say: "*Mea* culpa, *mea* culpa, *mea* maxima culpa." At last we are fully conscious of the two great realities of human life: the soul and God.

—*Lift Up Your Heart,* 164

Invasion of Divinity

When humans feel the first impulses of God's grace summoning them from misery to peace, they are sometimes inclined to shrug their shoulders and say: "This impulse to surrender does not come to me from any God; it is just a weakness of my human nature." Yet this explanation is patently untrue, because when God begins to affect the soul, it breaks with nature. A love of God inspires us to discipline and mortification, to give up the occasion of our sins. If the impulses were from nature alone, nature would not thus lift the knife against itself. Some opponents of religion say the experience of God is a projection of something we ourselves create in the subconscious mind. But there is nothing in the unconsciousness that was not once in consciousness;[1]

and here the soul is in the presence of a great Inexperience, a Divine Novelty, never known or even suspected before. Furthermore, when once the impulse of God strikes the soul it moves us to behavior contrary to either our conscious or our unconscious previous plans. This could not be if there were not present a Force from without, stronger than ourselves, and yet One with which we could cooperate. There is no need to multiply the answers to these false objections people raise against God. For there will always be perverse souls in the world who persist in disbelief, no matter what evidence is offered them. Their determination to deny love is very great, and they will go out of their way to find elaborate denials of the beautiful Obvious—as if someone were to try to dissuade us from enjoying the fragrance of a rose by saying that it really originated from a distant perfume factory.

The invasion of Divinity is a valid and unmistakable reality. Its effects are contentment with what we are and a yearning to be what we are not; it thus implies that a response is expected of us. No gift or favor ever has to be accepted, but once we consent to a favor, this creates an obligation. A refusal to respond to grace, at such a crisis, always leaves the soul more empty and bereft than ever. It is no slight thing to bar God from our doors when He has urgently asked us to let Him enter.

—Lift Up Your Heart, 159–160

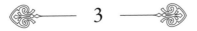

3

Hungry Heart

Our hunger for the infinite is never quieted; even those disillusioned by excess of pleasures have always kept in their imagination a hope of somewhere finding a truer source of satisfaction than any they have tried. Our search for the never-ending love is never ended—no one could really love anything unless he thought of it as eternal. Not everyone gives a name to this infinity toward which he tends and for which he yearns, but it is what the rest of us call God.

The pursuit of pleasure is thus a token of man's[1] higher nature, a symptom of his loneliness in this world. Torn between what he has, which surfeits him, and the far-off Transcendent, which attracts him, every worldly human being stands in grave danger of self-hatred and despair until he finds his true Infinite in God. As Pascal put it: "The knowledge of God without a perception of man's misery causes pride, and the knowledge of man's misery without perception of God causes despair. Knowledge of Jesus Christ constitutes the middle course, because in Him we find both God and our own misery."[2]

Until a person has discovered the true Infinite, he is invariably led from subjectivism—the setting up of his own ego as the absolute—to hedonism—the philosophy of a life given solely to sensate pleasures. . . .

The proper attitude toward life is not the one of pleasure seeking, but the cultivation of a Divine sense of humor within our human limitations. And what is humor? It is said that one has a sense of humor if he can "see the point" and that he lacks a sense of humor if "he cannot see the point." But God has made the world in such a way that He is the point of everything we see. The material is meant to be a revelation of the spiritual, the human a revelation of the Divine; and the fleeting experiences of our days, a revelation of Eternity. The universe, according to God's original plan, was made transparent, like a windowpane: A mountain was not to be just a mountain, but a symbol of the power of God. A snowflake was not just a snowflake, but a clue to the purity of God. Everything created was to tell something about God, for "by the visible things of the world is the Invisible God made manifest."[3] According to this plan, every person was to be a poet, a humorist, someone endowed with a sense of the invisible, infinite values in everything.

—Lift Up Your Heart, 53–54

The Cross

The Cross was the reason of His coming; now He made it the earmark of his followers. He did not make Christianity easy; for He implied not only must there be a voluntary renouncement of everything that hindered likeness with Him, but also there must be the suffering, shame, and death of the Cross. They did not have to blaze a trail of sacrifice themselves, but merely to follow His tracks zealously as the Man of Sorrow. No disciple is called to the task that is untried. He had taken the Cross first. Only those who were willing to be crucified with Him could be saved by the merits of His death, and only those who bore a Cross could ever really understand Him.

There was no question of whether or not men would have sacrifice in their lives; it was only a question of which they would sacrifice, the higher or the lower life!

> He who tries to save his life will lose it;
>> It is the man who loses his life
> For My sake, that will save it. (Luke 9:24)

If the physical, natural, and biological life was saved for pleasure, then the higher life of the spirit would be lost, but if the higher life of the spirit was chosen for salvation, then the lower or physical life had to be submitted to the Cross and self-discipline. There might be some natural virtues without a Cross, but there would never be a growth in virtue without it.

Cross-bearing, He then explained, was based on exchange. Exchange implies something that one can get along without, and something one cannot get along without. A man can get along without a dime, but he cannot get along without the bread which the dime will buy; so he exchanges one for another. Sacrifice does not mean "giving up" something, as if there were a loss; rather it is an exchange, an exchange of lower values for higher joys. But nothing in all the world is worth a soul.

> How is a man the better for it
>> If he gains the whole world
> At the expense of losing his own soul?

For a man's soul, what price can be high enough?
(Mark 8:39)

—Life of Christ, 225–226

 5

Grace

It is a fear of how grace *will* change and improve them that keeps many souls away from God. They want God to take them as they are and to let them stay that way. They want Him to take away their love of riches, but not their riches—to purge them of the disgust of sin, but not of the pleasure of sin. Some of them equate goodness with indifference to evil and think that God is good if He is broad-minded or tolerant about evil. Like the onlookers at the Cross, they want God on their terms, not His, and they shout, "Come down, and we will believe."[1] But the things they ask are the marks of a *false* religion: It promises salvation without a cross, abandonment without sacrifice, Christ without His nails. God is a consuming fire; our desire for

God must include a willingness to have the chaff burned from our intellect and the weeds of our sinful will purged. The very fear souls have of surrendering themselves to the Lord with a cross is an evidence of their instinctive belief in His Holiness. Because God is Fire, we cannot escape Him, whether we draw near for conversion or flee from aversion: In either case, He affects us. If we accept His love, its fires will illumine and warm us; if we reject Him, they will still burn on in us in frustration and remorse.

As all human beings are touched by God's flaming love, so also are all touched by the desire for His intimacy. No one escapes this longing; we are all kings in exile, miserable without the Infinite. Those who reject the grace of God have a desire to *avoid* God, as those who accept it have a desire *for* God. The modern atheist does not disbelieve because of his intellect, but because of his will.

—*Peace of Soul*, 241–242

HUMAN FREEDOM

[God] never forces our love. The surrender of the will to God is an all-important conversion because of this: God will not destroy our human freedom.

—Peace of Soul, 242

6

Authentic Freedom

When someone has . . . made the orbit of his life a movement around Christ, the thoughts he thinks, the desires that inflame him, the motivation of all his actions is centered in Our Divine Lord. The I still remains, but, as the Our Father suggests that it should be, the I is secondary— "*Thy* Will be done on earth as it is in Heaven." Such surrender is the peak of the I's activity—it is the I fulfilling itself by a free gift of self-will. For the one thing that is so much our own that God never impairs it is our freedom; the ability to sin is freedom's temporal and negative sign. As hell is its eternal and negative sign. And since the will is always free, it is the one supreme gift we can make to God. Such yielding of the center of our lives to Christ is the way of supreme happiness. Our happiness varies according to the center about which our lives revolve. If it is the ego, there are frustrations; if it is the I, there is a measure of natural happiness, still incomplete. If it is the Divine, there is the joy of being one with Infinite Life and Truth and Love.

The choice of the center rests with us: We must be satellites, serving some center, but we may choose our sun. We cannot remain in isolation from all centers: Every person gives away his freedom. Some give it to public opinion; some become the slaves of their own passions; some give away their freedom to dictators or the state, but some give their freedom away to God. Only in the last sort of surrender does one become truly free, for only then is one united with Him Whose will is our content. Public opinion, dictators, flesh, alcohol, when we serve them, never try to set us free, but our free will is a primary concern of the Divine: "If it is the Son Who makes you free men, you will have freedom in the earnest" (John 8:36).

—*Lift Up Your Heart*, 11–12

7

Sanctifying the Moment

Those who love God do not protest, whatever He may ask of them, nor doubt His kindness when He sends them difficult hours. A sick person takes medicine without asking the physician to justify its bitter taste, because he trusts the doctor's knowledge; so the soul that has sufficient faith accepts all the events of life as gifts from God, in the serene assurance that He knows best.

Every moment brings us more treasures than we can gather. The great value of the Now, spiritually viewed, is that it carries a message God has directed personally to us. Books, sermons, and broadcasts on a religious theme have the appearance of being circular letters, meant for everyone. Sometimes, when such general appeals do appear to have a personal application, the soul gets angry and writes vicious letters to allay its uneasy conscience: Excuses can always be found for ignoring the Divine Law.

But though moral and spiritual appeals carry God's identical message to all who listen, this is not true of the Now-moment; no one else but *I* am in exactly these circumstances; no one else has to carry the same burden, whether it be a sickness, the death of a loved one, or some other adversity. Nothing is more individually tailored to our spiritual needs than the Now-moment; for that reason it is an occasion of knowledge that can come to no one else. This moment is my school, my textbook, my lesson. Not even Our Lord disdained to learn from His specific Now; being God, He knew all, but there was still one kind of knowledge He could experience as a man. Saint Paul[1] describes it: "Son of God though He was, He learned obedience in the school of suffering" (Hebrews 5:8).

The University of the Moment has been built uniquely for each of us, and in comparison with the revelation God gives each in it, all other methods of learning are shallow and slow. This wisdom is distilled from intimate experience, is never forgotten; it becomes part of our character, our merit, our eternity. Those who sanctify the moment and offer it up in union with God's will never become frustrated—never grumble or complain. They overcome all obstacles by making them occasions of prayer and channels of merit. What were constrictions are thus made opportunities for growth. It is the modern pagan who is the victim of circumstance, and not its master. Such a person, having no practical knowledge of God, no trust in his Providence, no assurance of His Love, lacks the shock absorber of Faith and Hope and Love when difficult days come to him. His mind is caught within the pincers of a past he regrets or resents and a future he is afraid he cannot control. Being thus squeezed, his nature is in pain.

The one who accepts God's will in all things escapes such frustration by piercing the disguise of outward events to penetrate to their real character as messengers of the God he loves. It is strange how differently we accept misfortune—or even an insult—when we know who gave it to us. A teen might normally resent it very much if a well-dressed young woman accidentally stepped on her toes in a streetcar; but if that same teen recognized that the one who hurt her was her favorite movie star, she would probably boast of it to her friends. Demands that might seem outrageous from an acquaintance are met with happy compliance if it is a friend who asks our help. In like manner, we are able to adapt with a good grace to the demands of every Now when we recognize God's will and purpose behind the illness and the shocks and disappointments of life.

—*Lift Up Your Heart*, 210–212

8

Obedience

Inasmuch as the most general sin of mankind is pride or the exaltation of the ego, it was fitting that in atoning for that pride, Christ should practice obedience. He was not like one who is obedient for the sake of a reward, or in order to build up his character for the future; rather, being the Son, He already enjoyed the love of the Father to the full. It was out of this very fullness that there flowed a childlike surrender to His Father's will. He gave this as the reason for His surrender to the Cross. Within an hour or so before going into His agony in the Garden, He would say:

> The world must be convinced that I love the Father,
>> And act only as the Father has commanded Me to act.
>>> (John 14:30–31)

The only acts of Christ's childhood which are recorded are acts of obedience—obedience to His Heavenly Father and to His earthly parents. The foundation of obedience to man, He taught, is obedience to God. The elders who serve not God find that the young serve them not. His whole life was submission. He submitted to John's baptism, though He did not need it; He submitted to the temple tax, though as the Son of the Father, He was exempt from it; and He bade His followers to submit to Caesar. Calvary cast its shadow over Bethlehem; so now it darkened the obedient years at Nazareth. In being subject to creatures, though He was God, He prepared Himself for that final obedience—obedience to the humiliation of the Cross.

—*Life of Christ*, 54–55

9

Relief from Anxiety
and Trust in God

L ove is reciprocal; it is received in proportion as it is given. We generally trust only those who trust us; that is why there is a special Providence for those who trust God. Contrast two children, one child in a happy family, well provided with food, clothing, and education, the other a homeless orphan of the streets. The first child lives in an area of love; the second is outside of that area and enjoys none of its privileges. Many souls deliberately choose to exclude themselves from the area of the Heavenly Father's love where they might live as His children. They trust only their own resourcefulness, their own bank account, their own devices. This is particularly true of many families, who consider the rearing of children as solely an economic problem, never once invoking the Heavenly Father's Love: They are like a son who in time of need never called on his wealthy father for assistance. The result is they lose many of the blessings reserved for those who throw themselves into the loving arms of God. This law applies to nations as well as individuals.... Many favors and blessings are hanging from heaven to relieve our temporal anxieties if we would only cut them down with the sword of our trust in God. Relief from all wrong anxiety comes not from giving ourselves to God by halves, but by an all-encompassing love, wherein we go back, not to the past in fear or to the future in anxiety; but lie quietly in His hand having no will but His.

—*Peace of Soul*, 29

 10

Fiat

In the fullness of time an Angel of Light came down from the great Throne of Light to a Virgin kneeling in prayer, to ask her if she was willing to give God a human nature. Her answer was that she "knew not man" and, therefore, could not be the mother of the "Expected of the Nations."

There can never be a birth without love. In this the maiden was right. The begetting of new life requires the fires of love. But besides the human passion which begets life, there is the "passionless passion and wild tranquility"[1] of the Holy Spirit; and it was this that overshadowed the woman and begot in her Emmanuel or "God with us." At the moment that Mary pronounced *Fiat* or "Be it done," something greater happened than the *Fiat lux* (Let there be light) of creation; for the light that was now made was not the sun, but the Son of God in the flesh. By pronouncing *Fiat,* Mary achieved the full role of womanhood, namely, to be the bearer of God's gifts to man. There is a passive receptiveness in which woman says *Fiat* to the cosmos as she shares its rhythm, *Fiat* to a man's love as she receives it, and *Fiat* to God as she receives the Spirit.

—*Life of Christ,* 8–9

— 11 —

Vocation

No true vocation starts with "what I want" or with "a work I would like to do." If we are called by God, we may be sent to a work we do not like, and "obedience is better than sacrifice." If society calls, I can stop service; if Christ calls, I am a servant forever. If I feel my call is sociological dedication, there is no reason why I should enter a theological seminary. If I am convinced that a vocation is to be identified with the world, then I have completely forgotten Him Who warned: "I have taken you out of the world."[1]

The first stage in a vocation is a sense of the holiness of God. When Isaiah went into the Temple he had a vision of the Lord seated upon His throne, with angelic choirs singing:

Holy, holy, holy is the Lord of Hosts;
The whole earth is full of His glory.[2]

Vocation begins not with "what *I* would like to do" but with God. One is confronted with a presence, not as dramatic as Paul when he was converted, but with a sense of the unworldly, the holy and transcendent.

The second stage, which is a reaction to this, is a profound sense of unworthiness. The heart is shocked at the simultaneous vision of the clay and the treasure. God is holy, I am not. "Woe is me." God can do something with those who see what they really are and who know their need of cleansing, but can do nothing with the man who feels himself worthy.

—*Treasure in Clay*, 35

DIVINE LOVE

Divine love when it enters a soul (or, better, when we permit it to enter) takes possession of it, refreshes it, penetrates it utterly.

—*Lift Up Your Heart*, 238

 12

Beyond the Human

Love on the Divine level is very different from love on the purely human level, and sometimes there is conflict between the two. Our Divine Lord warned us that those who loved him would be hated. . . . ". . . It is because you do not belong to the world, because I have singled you out from the midst of the world, that the world hates you" (John 15:19). He also said that He came to bring not peace, but the sword, and that He would "set a man at variance with his father, and the daughter with her mother" (Matthew 10:35). There will always be those who can understand why love of a man or woman may be strong enough to make a lover cut all other ties but who consider it folly for anyone to fall in love with God and count the world well lost for Him.

Divine love when it enters a soul (or, better, when we permit it to enter) takes possession of it, refreshes it, penetrates it utterly. But it is as invisible as the wind, as mysterious as the falling of a meteor. It energizes what is slow to act; it strengthens what is feeble; it warms what is cold in us and makes even the bearing of our cross a joy. It removes all the boundaries that had been set by human love: It brings the Samaritan into the confines of the family. There is now neither Greek nor Pole, Russian nor Jew, German nor Frenchman, Japanese nor Chinese; they are all enfranchised to the realm of Divine Charity. It eliminates all limits on forgiveness, for when Our Lord said: "I tell thee to forgive, not seven wrongs, but seventy times seven" (Matthew 18:22), He did not mean four hundred and ninety, but a number beyond all mathematical count. Love travels far beyond mere forbearance, mere "goodness within reason." If someone forces us to walk one mile with him to punish us, Our Lord suggests that we walk with him yet another, to punish ourselves and thus come closer to the sinlessness God wants in us. Love is always ready to exceed common sense—Magdalene poured out all the ointment,[1] for love knows no limits.

—*Lift Up Your Heart*, 238–239

13

Mother of the Divine

Since men are unprepared for a revelation of the heavenly image of Love, which is Christ Jesus Our Lord, God, in His mercy, has prepared on earth an image of love that is not Divine but can lead to the Divine. Such is the role of His Mother. She can lift the fear, because her foot crushed the serpent of evil; she can do away with dread, because she stood at the foot of the Cross when human guilt was washed away and we were reborn in Christ.

As Christ is the Mediator between God and man, so she is the Mediatrix between Christ and us. She is the earthly principle of love that leads to the Heavenly Principle of Love. The relation between her and God is something like the relation between rain and the earth. Rain falls from the heavens, but the earth produces. Divinity comes from Heaven; the human nature of the Son of God comes from her. We speak of "mother earth," since it gives life through Heaven's gift of the sun; then why not also recognize the Madonna of the World, since she gives us the Eternal Life of God?

Those who lack faith are to be recommended particularly to Mary as a means to finding Christ, the Son of God. Mary, the Madonna of the World, exists where Christ is not yet and where the Mystical Body is not yet visible. . . .

She is grace where there is no grace; she is the Advent where there is no Christmas. In all lands where there is an ideal woman, or where virgins are venerated, or where one lady is set above all ladies, the ground is fertile for accepting the Woman as the prelude to embracing Christ. Where there is the presence of Jesus, there is the presence of His Mother; but where there is an absence of Jesus, through either ignorance or the wickedness of men, there is still the presence of Mary.

—*World's First Love*, 198–199

14

Perfect Love

Earthly love that is only the quest is incomplete; love that is only attainment is inert. If love is limited to possession, the beloved is absorbed and destroyed; if love is limited to only desire, it is a useless force that burns itself out as a spent star. This failure of either search or satisfaction to satisfy causes the mystery and sometimes the pain of love.

As pursuit alone, love is death by hunger; as satisfaction alone, love is death by satiety and its own "too much." If love could reach no higher than earth, it would be like the pendulum of a clock alternating and ticking away between chase to capture, capture to chase, endlessly. But our hearts crave something more. We long for an escape from this weary iteration of pursuit to capture; we do not wish in love to emulate the hunter who starts for new prey only because he has already killed the old.

And there is an escape. It lies in the eternal moment that combines both search and finding. In Heaven we shall capture Eternal Love, but an infinity of chase will not be enough to sound its depths. This is the Love in which you at last may have yourself and lose yourself in one and the same eternal now. Here the tension of romance and marriage is reconciled in an eternal instant of joy, an instant that would break the heart were it not that Love is life. Never to thirst would be inhuman, ever to thirst would be hell; but to drink and thirst in the same eternal now is to rise to the highest bliss of Love. This is the Love we "fall just short of in all love, the Beauty that leaves all other beauty in pain, the unpossessed that makes possession vain."[1] The closest we can come to such experience in our earthly imagination is to think of the most ecstatically happy moment of our lives—and then to live that moment eternalized. This kind of love would be speechless and ineffable; there could be no adequate expression of its ecstasies. That is why the love of God is called the Holy Spirit, the Holy Breath, something that is too deep for words.

It takes not two, but three to make perfect Love, whether it be in the flesh (husband, wife, and child), or in the spirit (lover, beloved, and love), or in Divine Nature (Father, Son, and Holy Spirit). Sex is duality; Love is always triune.

It is this fullness of Love that every heart in the universe wants. Some suspect it not, because they have never lifted the blind of their dark hearts to let in the light of God; others have been robbed of the hope by those who cannot think of love in any other terms than the concourse of two monkeys; others draw back from it in foolish fear lest, having the Flames of Love Divine, they may lose the dying embers of their present perverted desires. But others see that, as the golden streaks across the waters of the lake are reflections of the moon above, so human love is but the crushed-out reflection of the Heart Divine. In God alone is the consummation of all desires.

—*Peace of Soul*, 165–166

 — 15 —

The Mystery of Sex

If love does not climb, it falls. If, like the flame, it does not burn upward to the sun, it burns downward to destroy. If sex does not mount to heaven, it descends into hell. There is no such thing as giving the body without giving the soul. Those who think they can be faithful in soul to one another, but unfaithful in body, forget that the two are inseparable. Sex in isolation from personality does not exist! An arm living and gesticulating apart from the living organism is an impossibility. Man has no organic functions isolated from his soul. There is involvement of the whole personality. Nothing is more psychosomatic than the union of two in one flesh; nothing so much alters a mind, a will, for better or worse. The separation of soul and body is death. Those who separate sex and spirit are rehearsing for death. The enjoyment of the other's personality through one's own personality is love. The pleasure of animal function through another's animal function is sex separated from love.

Sex is one of the means God has instituted for the enrichment of the personality. It is a basic principle of philosophy that there is nothing in the mind that was not previously in the senses. All our knowledge comes from the body.[1] . . . Just as the enrichment of the mind comes from the body and its senses, so the enrichment of love comes through the body and its sex. As one can see a universe mirrored in a tear on a cheek, so in sex can be seen mirrored that wider world of love. Love in monogamous marriage includes sex; but sex, in the contemporary use of the term, does not imply either marriage or monogamy. . . .

But when sex is divorced from love there is a feeling that one has been stopped at the vestibule of the castle of pleasure; that the heart has been denied the city after crossing the bridge. Sadness and melancholy result from such a frustration of destiny, for it is the nature of man to be sad when he is pulled outside himself, or exteriorized, without getting any nearer his goal. There is a closer correlation between mental instability and the animal view of sex than many suspect. Happiness consists in interiority of the spirit, namely, the development of personality in relationship to a heavenly destiny. He who has no purpose in life is unhappy; he who exteriorizes his life and is dominated, or subjugated, by what is outside himself, or spends his energy on the external without understanding its mystery, is unhappy to the point of melancholy. There is the feeling of being hungry after having eaten or of being disgusted with food, because it has nourished not the body, in the case of an individual, or another body, in the case of marriage. In the woman, this sadness is due to the humiliation of realizing that, where marriage is only sex, her role could be fulfilled by any other woman; there is nothing personal, incommunicable, and therefore nothing dignified. Summoned by her God-implanted nature to be ushered into the mysteries of life, which have their source in God, she is condemned to remain on the threshold as a tool or an instrument of pleasure alone and not as a companion of love. Two glasses that are empty cannot fill up one another. There must be a fountain of water outside the glasses, in order that they may have communion with one another. It takes three to make love.

Every person is what *he* loves. Love becomes like unto that which it loves. If it loves heaven, it becomes heavenly; if it loves the carnal as a god, it becomes corruptible. The kind of immorality we have depends on the kind of loves we have. Putting it negatively, he who tells you what he does not love, also tells you what he is. "*Amor pondus meum*: Love is my gravitation," said Saint Augustine.[2] This slow conversion of a subject into an object, of a lover into the beloved, of the miser into his gold, of the saint into his God, discloses the importance of loving the right things. The nobler our loves, the nobler our character. To love what is below the human is degradation; to love what is human for the sake of the human is mediocrity; to love the human for the sake of the Divine is enriching; to love the Divine for its own sake is sanctity.

—*Three to Get Married*, 2–4

16

What the Heart Wants

The human heart was made for the Sacred Heart of Love, and no one but God can satisfy it. The heart is right in wanting the infinite; the heart is wrong in trying to make its finite companion the substitute for the infinite. The solution of the tension is in seeing that the disappointments it brings are so many reminders that one is on pilgrimage to Love.

Both the being loved too much and the being loved too little can go together when seen in the light of God. When the longing for infinite love is envisaged as a yearning for God, then the finiteness of the earthly love is seen as a reminder that "Our hearts were made for Thee, O Lord, and they can be satisfied only in Thee."[1]

The tug between what is immediate and what is interior now vanishes, as the very enjoyment that the immediacy of the flesh gives becomes the occasion for joy in the interiority of the soul, which knows that one is using it for God's purposes and for the salvation of both souls. The synthesis of life is achieved when the instincts are integrated to spirit and made useful to the ideals of the spirit. There is for the Christian no such thing in marriage as choosing between body and soul or sex and love. He must choose both together. Marriage is a vocation to put God in every detail of love. In this way, the dream of the bride and groom for eternal happiness really comes true, not in themselves alone, but through themselves. Now they love each other not as they dreamed they would, but as God dreamed they would. Such a reconciliation of the tension is possible only to those who know that it takes three to make love.

Only God can give what the heart wants. In true Christian love, the husband and wife see God coming *through* their love. But without God the infinity must be sought in the finitude of the partner, which is to gather figs from thistles. Eternity is in the soul, and all the materialism of the world cannot uproot it. The tragedy of the materialist psychologies of our day comes from trying to make a bodily function satisfy the infinite aspirations of the soul. It is this that creates complexes and unstable minds and divorce courts. It is like trying to put all the words of a book on the cover. Eliminate the Divine Third from human love and there is left only the substitution of cruel repetition for infinity. The need for God never disappears. Those who deny the existence of water are still thirsty, and those who deny God still want Him in their craving for Beauty and Love and Peace, which He alone is.

—*Three to Get Married*, 31–32

 17

Divine Mercy

[Jesus] gave up His spirit to show that His love was stronger than death. Blood and water came forth; Blood, the price of Redemption and the symbol of the Eucharist; water, the symbol of regeneration and baptism. Saint John, who witnessed the scene of the soldier piercing the Heart of Christ, wrote about it later:

> He it is, Jesus Christ, Whose coming
>> Has been made known to us by water and blood;
> Water and blood as well, not water only. (1 John 5:6)

There was something more than a natural phenomenon here, inasmuch as John gave it a mysterious and sacramental significance. Water stood at the beginning of our Lord's ministry when He was baptized, Blood stood at the close of it when He offered Himself as a spotless oblation. Both became the ground of faith, for at the baptism, the Father declared Him to be His Son, and the Resurrection witnessed again to His Divinity.

The messenger from the Father was impaled with the message of love written on His Own Heart. The thrust of the lance was the last profanation of God's Good Shepherd. Though He was spared the brutality that was arbitrary, such as the breaking of His legs, nevertheless, there was some mysterious Divine purpose in the opening of the Sacred Heart of God. John, who leaned on His breast the night of the Last Supper, fittingly recorded the opening of the Heart. At the Deluge Noah made a door in the side of the ark, by which the animals entered, that they might escape the flood; now a new door is opened into the heart of God into which men might escape the flood of sin. When Adam slept, Eve was taken from his side and was called the mother of all the living. Now as the second Adam inclined His head and slept on the Cross under the figure of Blood and water there came from His side His bride, the Church.

—*Life of Christ*, 579

SIN

It is so easy to lose Christ; He can be lost by even a little heedlessness; a little want of watchfulness, and the Divine presence slips away. . . . Sin is the loss of Jesus.

—*The World's First Love,* 218

 18

Death of Selfishness

Purification rids us of the dead weight of evil habits and the ballast of the flesh. The soul then becomes more and more free, and derives a greater pleasure than it ever guessed was possible. As Saint Thomas says: "Men must have pleasures. If they will not have joys of the spirit, then they will degenerate into pleasure of the body."[1] Unless there is some other interest to compensate for the loss of a surrendered pleasure, minds become cynical and bitter with an increasing desire to be coddled, respected, honored, and made the center of attention. Egotists find it hard to change, because the egotist refuses to postpone satisfaction. Overfed, overupholstered, double-chinned, he refuses to accept a few moments of pain through self-control—and thus misses a joy in this life and an eternal life beyond. A life of detachment, looked at from the outside, seems a *living death*, but once begun it is found to be a *dying life*; for each new death of selfishness, like the seed falling to the ground, brings forth a corresponding life. There are no shortcuts to spirituality; pain and purification go hand in hand, for sin is not easily discarded. Purification never means crushing our wills in order to become will-less; but the will, detached from the dead weight of sin, more readily flies to union with the Will Divine. When one gets down to rock bottom, one soon discovers that the principal reason souls do not come to God is not only because they are ignorant, but because they are also bad; it is their behavior that creates the biggest obstacle to belief, however vigorously they deny it. "You will not come to Me to find life" (John 5:40). Associated with this reluctance toward sacrifice is an unwillingness to renounce pride and a refusal to immolate the heart. This absence of humility and sacrificial love stands like a wall between the soul and God; when it hears the Divine Command, it pleads to God, Who was similarly rejected by the man who bought a farm, "Have me excused, O Lord."[2]

But this reluctance is not universal. Many weary souls would come to God if the faith were presented to them the hard way instead of the easy way: by an appeal to self-sacrifice rather than an appeal to understanding. There is a far greater readiness for sacrifice on the part of the modern mind than some members of Christ's Mystical Body perceive. The good qualities of the modern soul have been underestimated and many would be surprised at its reaction, if shown the pierced Hands and Feet of Christ and asked: "How did They get that way?" There is a greater yearning for sacrifice in the hearts and minds of men and women than at any time in the last five hundred years. Whence came the heroism of soldiers during the war—at a time when we all were supposed to have been softened by luxury and ease—if it was not because this potential for sacrifice was always there in the depths of their hearts? The world is now tired of a broad-mindedness that is as cold as a miser's heart and as spineless as a filet of sole; it wants to catch fire, to feel the burning heat of its passions, and, above all, to love even to the point of death.

—*Lift Up Your Heart*, 117–118

19

Self-Discipline

Occasion of sin means those places and persons and circumstances that constitute the environment favorable to the development of self-love. For the alcoholic, it might be a bar, a certain home, or a boon companion; for the erotic, a certain person; for the scandalmonger, a gossip who always has scandal to trade. As a wise and cautious traveler, looking ahead, avoids obstacles in his path, so the person who is on the way to heaven deliberately avoids those things that interfere with the development of his character and union with God. Many a soul who once had faith and lost it, and many who no longer have well-integrated personalities in the natural order, can trace their loss of peace of soul and peace of mind to evil companionship or to an environment that robbed them of their heritage. Sacred Scripture warns us that "he that loveth danger shall perish in it."[1]

. . . *Love* is a yearning for a person or thing that delights and pleases us; and when we love, we crave either possession or unity. *Hatred* is only love upside down. All hatred is born of love, because we hate that which in any way endangers our love. For example, we hate disease because we love health, and hatred is, at bottom, an eagerness to rid ourselves of whatever displeases us. *Desire* is an urge or quest for an absent good, and it is born of love for another good, which may be a thing or person. *Aversion* is the passion that makes us shun or repel some proximate or approaching evil, and *joy* is the passion of satisfaction that arises from the present possession of any good. *Sadness* is grief over an evil or disaster that is present. *Courage* or *daring* is the passion that makes us strive after some lovable good, whose possession is difficult or arduous. *Despair* is the passion that arises in the soul when possession or union with the loved object seems impossible. Finally, *anger* is the passion that violently repels what hurts us and incites in us the desire for revenge.

It need hardly be repeated that all of these passions, when well ordered, are God-given. Our Blessed Lord experienced many of them. Not only did He love us with His Whole Will and His Whole Heart, but He also wept over the city of Jerusalem and shed tears at the death of Lazarus; He aroused himself to righteous indignation and anger when

He drove the buyers and the sellers out of the Temple; He felt fear and anxiety when He went into the Garden of Gethsemane, and yet all of these passions were so disciplined that they were used to purchase our salvation.

—*Lift Up Your Heart*, 109–111

20

Egotism

Egotism—an inordinate love of self—is the basic cause of all sins and of all unhappiness that lacks a rational cause. There are also other effects of self-love, so numerous that no psychologist has ever listed them in their completeness. Fear, for instance, is an isolation from our neighbor, a feeling that we are surrounded by foes bent on the destruction of our ego. Procrastination is the act of an ego refusing to face its responsibilities in order to enjoy its ease. Worrying about other people and "bossing" them result when the ego is trying to maintain itself as a center of the cosmos. The bore is the egotist struggling to increase his prestige, either by telling about the books he has read or the women he has wooed. Cursing is an art of the ego in rebellion against the God

Who challenges its superiority or renders the ego in wild pursuit of attention. . . . Defiance of the ordinary standards of society results if the ego sets itself above the rest of the people. In the spoiled child's tantrums the youthful ego draws attention to itself. Hurry, hustle, [and] bustle . . . are the outward sacraments of an ego bent on impressing other people with its own superiority. The telling of stories at the expense of someone else reveals the ego in jealousy or in envy.

At the root of every such disorder is self-love, the error in living, which hatches a brood of seven major effects of egotism. These—the seven pallbearers of character—are Pride, Avarice, Envy, Lust, Anger, Gluttony, Sloth. It is against these seven major forms of egotism that self-knowledge is directed.

—*Lift Up Your Heart*, 83–84

Examining Oneself

It is not true that acknowledging our sins as sins induces a guilt complex or morbidity. Because a child goes to school, does he or she develop an ignorance complex? Because the sick go to the doctor, do they have a sickness complex? The student concentrates, not upon his own ignorance, but upon the wisdom of the teacher; the sick concentrate not upon their illness, but upon the curative powers of the doctor; and the sinner, seeing his sins for what they are, concentrates not on his own guilt, but upon the redemptive powers of the Divine Physician. There is *no evidence whatever* to sustain the position of some psychiatrists that consciousness of sin tends to make a person morbid. To call someone an escapist because he asks God for forgiveness is like calling a householder whose home is on fire an escapist because he sends for the fire department. If there is anything morbid in the sinner's responsible admission of a violated relationship with Divine Love, this is a jovial sanity compared with the real and terrible morbidity that comes to those who are sick and refuse to admit their illness. The greatest refinement of pride, the most contemptible form of escapism, is to refrain from examining oneself, lest sin be discovered within.

As a drunkard will sometimes become conscious of the gravity of his intemperance only through the startling vision of how much he has wrecked his own home and the wife who loved him, so, too, sinners may come to an understanding of their wickedness when they understand what they have done to Our Divine Lord. That is why the Cross has always played a central part in the Christian picture. It brings out what is worst in us by revealing what sin can do to goodness and love. It brings out the best in us by revealing what goodness can do for sin—forgive and atone at the moment of sin's greatest cruelty. The Cross of Christ does something for us that we cannot do for ourselves. Everywhere else in the world we are spectators; but, facing the vision of the Cross, we pass from spectatorship to participation. If anyone thinks that the confession of his guilt is escapism, let him try once kneeling at the foot of the Crucifix. He cannot escape feeling involved. One look at Christ on the Cross, and the scab is torn from the ulcerous depths of sin as it stands revealed in all of its ugliness. Just one flash of that Light of the World shatters all the blindness that sins have begotten and burns into the soul the truth of our relationship to God. Those who have refused to go up to Calvary are those who do not weep for their sins. Once a soul has gone there, it can no longer say that sin does not matter.

—*Peace of Soul,* 79–81

22

Confession

If a piece of glass gets into the hand, the hand will first try to expel it by bleeding; when it cannot get rid of the glass, it then proceeds to surround the glass with fibrous tissue to prevent it from harming the rest of the body. When the doctor later operates and digs out the piece of glass to prevent infection, he is doing what nature first intended, namely, preventing repression and its consequent irritation. In the moral order, Our Divine Lord said that repression of sins was dangerous; if we covered them up, they would cause an irritation with eternal consequences. So He asked His Apostles to go around the world preventing repression by hearing confessions and forgiving sins. Now psychiatry has seen the wisdom of doing for the diseased mind what doctors have done for the body and what religion has done for the soul from time immemorial—get a release, get a confession. . . .[1]

The spirit of confession is not one of fact-finding, but of mercy. If a human being accords pardon to others who humbly avow their faults, why should not God do the same? That is precisely what Our Blessed Lord has done. He has taken the natural avowal of faults—which already has an expiatory force—and has elevated it to the dignity of a Sacrament. Avowal is only human, but He has divinized it. What is natural, He has made supernatural. The indispensable condition of receiving human pardon—the open avowal of guilt—is the condition upon which Almighty God grants His pardon in the Sacrament of Mercy. With infinite tenderness, He told the story of the prodigal son who came back to his father, acknowledged his guilt, and was rewarded with the embrace and kiss of his father. Such is the joy of God at a sinner's return, for "even so there shall be joy in heaven upon one sinner that does penance, more than upon ninety-nine just who need not penance" (Luke 15:7).

—Peace of Soul, 120, 124

23

Perfect Sorrow

There are some men and women who, admitting their sins and faults, are still unhappy. Where there is a genuine sense of guilt, release can come only from Divine Mercy confronting human misery. Unless we are ready to ask for the forgiveness of our sins by God, the examination of conscience may be only a vain form of introspection, which can make a soul worse if it ends in *remorse* instead of *sorrow*. For the two are quite distinct: Judas had remorse. Peter had sorrow. Judas "repented unto himself," as Scripture tells us; Peter, unto the Lord. As a psychic malady sometimes results from a failure to adjust self to the right environment, so a moral evil results from the failure of the soul to adjust itself to God. Despair is such a failure—Judas despaired, but Peter hoped. Despair comes from unrelatedness, from the refusal of a soul to turn to God. Such a soul opposes the order of nature.

When there are seven people in a room, few ever refer to the fact that there are fourteen arms present. But if we found a detached arm lying in a corner, it would create consternation; it is a problem only because it is detached. A soul isolated from God is like that arm. Its conscience (to take another example) is like a broken anklebone; it hurts because it is not where it ought to be. The final stage of this sadness resulting from a person's unrelatedness to God is a desire to die, combined with a fear of death—for "conscience doth make cowards of us all."[1]

But if remorse is a sense of guilt unrelated to God, it is well to consider other states of mind and conscience from this single aspect. We find there are several classes of souls, ranged according to the degree of their relatedness to God. There are those who killed their conscience by sin and worldliness and who have steadfastly refused to cooperate with the Divine Action on the soul in order to amend their lives, confess their sins, and do penance; there are those who have awakened from a state of sin; there are those who followed conscience and the laws of God for a time and then turned away from God; and, finally, there are those who kept their baptismal innocence and never defiled their conscience. The second and the fourth classes are very dear to God. There are thus two ways of knowing how good God is: One is by never losing Him, and the other is by losing Him and finding Him again. Souls who have strayed and returned, Our Lord said, rejoice the Angels in Heaven more than the steadfastly faithful. This is not difficult to understand; a mother with ten children rejoices more in the recovery of the single sick child than in the continued possession of health by the other nine.

For the sinner to be made well, then, confession and sorrow are required. And the sorrow must have in it an appeal to God's mercy to distinguish it from remorse. Saint Paul makes the distinction in writing to the Corinthians: "For the sorrow that is according to God works penance, steadfast unto salvation; but the sorrow of the world works death" (2 Corinthians 7:10). Remorse, or "the sorrow of the world," results in worry, jealousy, envy, indignation; but sorrow related to God results in expiation and hope. Perfect sorrow comes from a sense of having offended God, Who is deserving of all our love; this sorrow or contrition, felt in confession, is never a vexing, fretful sadness that depresses, but it is a sadness from which great consolation springs.

—*Peace of Soul*, 193–194

24

Divine Physician

Human beings need to be put together more than they need to be taken apart. Sin divides us against ourselves; absolution restores our unity. Most people today have a load on their minds because they have a load on their consciences; the Divine Psychologist knew how miserable we should be if we could not unload that burden. Hospitals are built because people have sick bodies, and the Church builds confessional[s] . . . because they also have sick souls. . . . The Divine Master knew what is in humanity; so He instituted this Sacrament, not for His needs, but for ours. It was His way of giving us a happy heart. The left side of the physical heart and the right side of the heart have no direct communication with each other; they are joined through the medium of the blood circulating through the body. Our hearts become happy, too, by communicating with Christ's Mystical Body and His Blood. We are not made worse by admitting the need for absolution. We are not made worse even by admitting we are all brokenhearted; for unless our hearts are broken, how else could God get in?

—*Peace of Soul*, 140

KNOWING
JESUS

It [is] not enough to know the existence of God as proved by reason . . . eternal life comes only from knowing Jesus Christ.

—Life of Christ, 450

Where Divinity Is Found

In the filthiest place in the world, a stable, Purity was born. He, Who was later to be slaughtered by men acting as beasts, was born among beasts. He, Who would call Himself the "living Bread descended from Heaven,"[1] was laid in a manger, literally, a place to eat. Centuries before, the Jews had worshiped the golden calf, and the Greeks, the ass. Men bowed down before them as before God. The ox and the ass now were present to make their innocent reparation, bowing down before their God.

There was no room in the inn, but there was room in the stable. The inn is the gathering place of public opinion, the focal point of the world's moods, the rendezvous of the worldly, the rallying place of the popular and the successful.

But the stable is a place for the outcasts, the ignored, the forgotten. The world might have expected the Son of God to be born—if He was to be born at all—in an inn. A stable would be the last place in the world where one would have looked for Him. *Divinity is always where one least expects to find it.*

No worldly mind would ever have suspected that He Who could make the sun warm the earth would one day have need of an ox and an ass to warm Him with their breath; that He Who, in the language of Scriptures, could stop the turning about of Arcturus[2] would have His birthplace dictated by an imperial census; that He, Who clothed the fields with grass, would Himself be naked; that He, from Whose hands came planets and worlds, would one day have tiny arms that were not long enough to touch the huge heads of the cattle; that the feet which trod the everlasting hills would one day be too weak to walk; that the Eternal Word would be dumb; that Omnipotence would be wrapped in swaddling clothes; that Salvation would lie in a manger; that the bird which built the nest would be hatched therein—no one would ever have suspected that God coming to this earth would ever be so helpless. And that is precisely why so many miss Him. *Divinity is always where one least expects to find it.*

—*Life of Christ*, 16–17

The Good Shepherd

Men have existence, but [Jesus] would give them life, not biological or physical life, but Divine life. Nature suggests but cannot give this more abundant life. Animals have life more abundantly than plants; man has life more abundantly than animals. He said that He came to give a life beyond the human. As the oxygen could not live the more abundant life of the plant unless the plant came down to it, so neither could man share Divine Life unless Our Lord *came* down to give it.

Next, He proceeded to demonstrate that He gave this life not by His teaching, but by His dying. He was not uniquely a Teacher, but primarily a Savior. To illustrate again the purpose of His coming, He reached back into the Old

Testament. No figure is more often employed in the Exodus to describe God leading His people from slavery to freedom than that of a shepherd. The prophets also often spoke of the shepherds who preserved a flock in good pastures as distinct from false shepherds. God is depicted by Isaias[1] as carrying His sheep in His arms, and by Ezechiel as a shepherd looking for His lost sheep. Zecharias gave the saddest picture of all in prophesying that the Messiah-shepherd would be struck, and the sheep dispersed. Best known is Psalm 23, where the Lord is pictured leading His sheep into green pastures.

The Lord revealed at what cost these green pastures are purchased. He was not the Good Shepherd because He provided economic plenty, but because He would lay down His life for His sheep. Once again the Cross appears under the symbol of the shepherd. The shepherd-patriarch Jacob and the shepherd-king David now pass into the Shepherd-Savior, as the staff becomes a crook, the crook a scepter, and the scepter a Cross.

—*Life of Christ*, 264–265

 27

The Sacrifice of the Mass

Picture a house [with] two large windows on opposite sides. One window looks down into a valley, the other to a towering mountain. The owner could gaze on both and somehow see that they were related: the valley is the mountain humbled; the mountain is the valley exalted.

The Sacrifice of the Mass is something like that. Every church, in a way, looks down on a valley, but the valley of death and humiliation in which we see a cross. But it also looks up to a mountain, an eternal mountain, the mountain of Heaven where Christ reigns gloriously. As the valley and mountain are related as humiliation and exaltation, so the Sacrifice of the Mass is related to Calvary in the valley, and to Christ in Heaven and the eternal hills.

All three, Calvary, the Mass, and the glorified Christ in heaven, are different levels of the great eternal act of love. The Christ Who appeared in Heaven as the lamb slain from the beginning of the world, at a certain moment in time, came to this earth and offered His Life in Redemption for the sins of men. Then He ascended into heaven where that same eternal act of love continues as He intercedes for humanity, showing the scars of His Love to His heavenly Father. True, agony and crucifixion are passing things, but the obedience and the love which inspired them are not. In the Father's eyes, the Son-made-Man loves always unto death. The patriot who regretted that he had only one life to give his country would have loved to have made his sacrifice eternal.[1] Being man, he could not do it. But Christ, being God and man, could.

The Mass, therefore, looks backward and forward. Because we live in time and can use only earthly symbols, we see successively that which is but one eternal movement of love. If a motion picture reel were endowed with consciousness, it would see and understand the story at once; but we do not grasp it until we see it unfolded upon the screen. So it is with the love by which Christ prepared for His coming in the Old Testament, offered Himself on Calvary, and now re-presents it in Sacrifice in the Mass. The Mass, therefore, is not another immolation but a new presentation of the eternal Victim and its application to us. To assist at Mass is the same as to assist at Calvary. But there are differences.

On the Cross, Our Lord offered Himself for all mankind; in the Mass we make application of that death to ourselves, and unite our sacrifice with His. The disadvantage of not having lived at the time of Christ is nullified by the Mass. On the Cross, He *potentially* redeemed all humanity; in the Mass we actualize that Redemption. Calvary happened at a definite moment in time and on a particular hill in space. The Mass temporalizes and spatializes that eternal act of love.

The Sacrifice of Calvary was offered up in a bloody manner by the separation of His blood from His body. In the Mass, this death is mystically and sacramentally presented in an unbloody manner, by the separate consecration of the blood and wine. The two are not consecrated together by such words as "This is My Body and My Blood"; rather, following the words of our Lord: "This is My Body" is said over the bread; then "This is My Blood" is said over the wine. The separate consecration is a kind of mystical sword dividing body and blood, which is the way Our Lord died on Calvary.

Suppose there was an eternal broadcasting station that sent out eternal waves of wisdom and enlightenment. People who lived in different ages would tune in to that wisdom, assimilate it, and apply it to themselves. Christ's eternal act of love is something to which we tune in, as we appear in successive ages of history through the Mass. The Mass, therefore, borrows its reality and its efficacy from Calvary and has no meaning apart from it. He who assists at Mass lifts the Cross of Christ out of the soil of Calvary and plants it in the center of his own heart.

This is the only perfect act of love, sacrifice, thanksgiving, and obedience which we can ever pay to God; namely, that which is offered by His Divine Son Incarnate. Of and by ourselves, we cannot touch the ceiling because we are not tall enough. Of and by ourselves, we cannot touch God. We need a Mediator, someone who is both God and Man, Who is Christ. No human prayer, no human act of self-denial, no human sacrifice is sufficient to pierce Heaven. It is only the Sacrifice of the Cross that can do so, and this is done in the Mass. As we offer it, we hang, as it were, onto His robes, we tug at His feet at the Ascension, we cling to His pierced hands in offering Himself to the Heavenly Father. Being hidden in Him, our prayers and sacrifices have His value. In the Mass we are once more at Calvary, rubbing shoulders with Mary Magdalene and John, while mournfully looking over our shoulders at executioners who still shake dice for the garments of the Lord.

The priest who offers the Sacrifice merely lends to Christ his voice and his fingers. It is Christ Who is the priest; it is Christ Who is the Victim. In all pagan sacrifices and in the Jewish sacrifices, the victim was always *separate* from the priest. It might have been a goat, a lamb, or a bullock. But when Christ came, He the Priest offered Himself as the Victim. In the Mass, it is Christ Who still offers Himself and

Who is the Victim to Whom we become united. The altar, therefore, is not related to the congregation as the stage to an audience in the theater. . . . All the members of the Church have a kind of priesthood, inasmuch as they offer up with the Eternal Priest this eternal act of love. The laity participate in the life and power of Christ, for "Thou hast made us a royal race of priests to serve God."[2]

—*The Sacraments*, 73–74, 76

28

The Holy Hour

[Three reasons why Fulton Sheen recommends regularly spending an hour in prayer before the Eucharist]

First, the Holy Hour is not a devotion; it is a sharing in the work of redemption. . . . In the Garden, Our Lord contrasted two "hours"—one was the evil hour "this is your hour"—with which Judas could turn out the lights of the world. In contrast, Our Lord asked: "Could you not watch one hour with Me?"[1] In other words, He asked for an hour of reparation to combat the hour of evil; an hour of victimal union with the Cross to overcome the anti-love of sin.

Secondly, the only time Our Lord asked the Apostles for anything was the night He went into His agony. Then He did not ask *all* of them . . . perhaps because He knew He could not count on their fidelity. But at least He expected three to be faithful to Him: Peter, James, and John. As often in the history of the Church since that time, evil was awake, but the disciples were asleep. That is why there came out of His anguished and lonely Heart the sigh: "Could you not watch one hour with Me?" Not for an hour of activity did He plead, but for an hour of companionship.

The third reason [to pray a] Holy Hour is to grow more and more into His likeness. As Paul puts it: "We are transfigured into His likeness, from splendor to splendor."[2] We become like that which we gaze upon. Looking into a sunset, the face takes on a golden glow. Looking at the Eucharistic Lord for an hour transforms the heart in a mysterious way as the face of Moses was transformed after his companionship with God on the mountain. Something happens to us similar to that which happened to the disciples at Emmaus. On Easter Sunday afternoon when the Lord met them, He asked why they were so gloomy. After spending some time in His presence, and hearing again the secret of spirituality—"The Son of man must suffer to enter into His Glory"[3]—their time with Him ended, and their "hearts were on fire."[4]

—A Treasure in Clay, 197–198

29

Christ's Memorial

Bread must be broken; and He Who had come from God must be a sacrificial Victim, that men might truly feed on Him. Hence, it would be a Bread that would result from the voluntary offering of His own flesh to rescue the world from the slavery of sin unto the newness of life.

"And now what is this Bread which I am to give?
It is My Flesh, given for the life of the world.
Then the Jews fell to disputing with one another,
How can this Man give us His Flesh to eat?"
Whereupon Jesus said to them,
"Believe Me when I tell you this;
You can have no life yourselves,
Unless you eat the Flesh of the Son of Man,
And drink His Blood." (John 6:52–54)

He not only pictured Himself as One Who had come down from heaven but as One Who had come down to *give* Himself, or to die. It would only be in the slain Christ that they would come to understand the glory of a Bread that nourishes unto eternity. He was here referring to His death; for the word "giving" expressed the sacrificial act. The Flesh and Blood of the Incarnate Son of God, which would be severed in death, would become the source of everlasting life. When He said, "My Flesh," He meant His human nature, as "the Word became Flesh" meant that God the Word or the Son assumed to Himself a human nature. But it was only because that human nature would be linked to a Divine Personality for all eternity that He could give eternal life to those who received it. And when He said that He would give that for the life of the world, the Greek word used meant "all mankind."[1]

His words became more poignant because this was the season of the Passover. Though the Jews looked on blood in an awesome manner, they were leading their lambs at that time to Jerusalem, where blood would be sprinkled to the four directions of the earth. The strangeness of the utterance about giving His Body and Blood diminished against the background of the Passover; He meant that the shadow of the animal lamb was passing, and that its place was being taken by the true Lamb of God. As they had communion with the flesh and blood of the Paschal Lamb, so they would now have communion with the Flesh and Blood of the true Lamb of God. He Who was born in Bethlehem, the "House of Bread," and was laid in a manger, a place of food for lower animals, would now be to men, so inferior to Him, their Bread of Life. Everything in nature has to have communion in order to live; and through it what is lower is transformed into what is higher: chemical into plants, plants into animals, animals into man. And man? Should he not be elevated through communion with Him Who "came down"² from heaven to make man a partaker of the Divine nature? As a Mediator between God and man, He said that, as He lived by the Father, so they would live by Him:

> "As I live because of the Father,
>   The living Father Who has sent Me,
> So he who eats Me will live,
>   In his turn, because of Me." (John 6:58)

—*Life of Christ*, 183–185

 **30**

Road to Emmaus

At last [the two disciples and Jesus] arrived at Emmaus. [Jesus] made it appear as if He were about to continue His journey along the same road, just as once before when a storm was sweeping the lake, He made it appear as though He would pass by the boat of the Apostles. The two disciples begged Him, however, to stay with them. Those who have good thoughts of God in the day will not readily surrender them at nightfall. They had learned much, but they knew that they had not learned all. They still did not recognize Him, but there was a light about Him which promised to lead to a fuller revelation and dissipate their gloom. Their invitation to be a guest He accepted, but immediately He acted as the Host, for:

When He sat down at table with them,

    He took bread, and blessed, and broke it,

And offered it to them; whereupon their eyes

    Were opened, and they recognized Him;

And with that, He disappeared from their sight. (Luke 24:30, 31)

This taking of the bread and breaking it and giving it to them was not an ordinary act of courtesy, for it resembled too closely the Last Supper at which He bade His Apostles to repeat the Memorial of His death as He broke the bread which was His Body and gave it to them. Immediately on the reception of the Sacramental Bread that was broken, the eyes of their souls were opened. As the eyes of Adam and Eve were opened to see their shame after they had eaten the forbidden fruit of the knowledge of good and evil, so now the eyes of the disciples were opened to discern the Body of Christ. The scene parallels the Last Supper: in both there was a giving of thanks; in both, a looking up to heaven; in both, the breaking of the bread; and in both; the giving of the bread to the disciples. With the conferring of the bread came a knowledge which gave greater clarity than all the instructions. The breaking of the bread had introduced them into an experience of the glorified Christ. Then He disappeared from their sight. Turning to one another, they reflected:

"Were not our hearts burning within us

    When He spoke to us on the road,

And when He made the scriptures plain to us?" (Luke 24:32)

His influence on them was both affective and intellectual; affective, in the sense that it made their hearts burn with love; and intellectual, inasmuch as it gave them an understanding of the hundreds of preannouncements of His coming. Mankind is naturally disposed to believe that anything religious must be striking and powerful enough to overwhelm the imagination. Yet this incident on the road to Emmaus revealed that the most powerful truths often appear in the commonplace and trivial incidents of life, such as meeting a fellow traveler on a road. Christ veiled His Presence in the most ordinary roadway of life. Knowledge of Him came as they walked with Him; and the knowledge was that of glory that came through defeat. In His Glorified Life as in His public life, the Cross and glory went together. It was not just His teachings that were recalled; it was His sufferings and how expedient they were for His exaltation.

—*Life of Christ*, 604–606

 31

Power from on High

While on earth [Jesus] exercised the triple office of Priest, Prophet or Teacher, and King. Now as He prepared to leave them for heaven whence He came, He deputed that triple office to His Apostles: the priestly office in bidding them renew the Memorial of His death and by conferring on them the power to forgive sins; the prophetic or teaching office, by promising to send them the Spirit of Truth Who would recall to their minds all things He had taught them and would keep them one in faith; and the kingly office, by giving them a Kingdom (as His Father had given Him a Kingdom), over which they had the powers of binding and loosing. Leaving no doubt that the purpose of His coming was to prolong His Priesthood, His Truth, and His Kingship, He consigned His Apostles to the world:

"You therefore, must go out,
  Making disciples of all nations,
And baptizing them in the name of the Father
  And of the Son, and of the Holy Ghost,
Teaching them to observe all commandments
  Which I have given you." (Matthew 28:19, 20)

If this commission were given solely for the time span of the Apostles, it is evident that they could not possibly go to all nations. The dynamism or current that was passed into the Apostles under the headship of Peter was to continue until Christ's Second Coming. No doubt was left concerning the authority and the work of the Church when the Master would leave the earth. That day the Propagation of the Faith came into being. No longer were the Apostles and their successors to consider themselves solely as masters in Israel; from now on the whole world was theirs. Nor were they merely to teach; for He Who gave the commission was not just a teacher. They were to make disciples in every nation; and discipleship implied surrender of heart and will to the Divine Master. The power of His redemptive Cross would be in vain unless His servants used it to incorporate other human natures unto Himself. As Mary gave Him the human nature which was now glorified in His Person, so men were to give their human natures to Him, dying as He died, in order that they might enter into glory.

—*Life of Christ*, 631–632

Continuing in the School of Fulton J. Sheen

Now that you have entered the school of Fulton J. Sheen, you are part of his "posse!" If the words and wisdom of Bishop Sheen have inspired you and spoken to your heart, you may want to ponder more deeply all that you have read through continued meditation, journaling, discussion, and prayer with the following questions:

1. What piece of wisdom from Sheen spoke to your heart the most?

2. In what way did Sheen's teachings help you to better understand God and his personal love for you?

3. Is there one area of Sheen's teaching that you would like to apply to your own life?

4. Did Sheen's writings give you any insights into your own vocational path—be it married life, the priesthood, religious life, or single life?

5. Is there a particular problem or area of your life for which you feel inspired to seek Fulton Sheen's intercession?

6. If you could share Fulton Sheen's teaching and wisdom with someone in your life, who would that be and why?

Ex Libris

Fulton Sheen left a legacy of countless written works and hours of recorded radio and TV broadcasts. For this book, I chose content from seven of my favorite Sheen literary works. I pray that sitting at the feet of Venerable Fulton Sheen and reading these provocative excerpts have led you deeper on your journey with Christ.

In case you are interested in reading further, I am sharing more information on the sources used for this compilation. I pray you have been blessed and encourage you to go deeper with the Lord and his saints.

Three to Get Married

As I mentioned in the introduction, this was the first work I read from Fulton Sheen. It is a timely work for today's culture that in many ways has abandoned and forgotten the beauty of marriage. This brilliant and timeless book should be on everyone's bedside table, especially those who are praying for a spouse, all preparing for this great Sacrament, and all those living the Sacrament. Your views on marriage will be transformed upon reading *Three to Get Married*.

Life of Christ

This book provides a close encounter with Jesus in a way that takes the Gospels to another level. *Life of Christ* should truly be on a bookshelf in every Christian household and religious education formation program. If you want to enhance your understanding of Jesus, Sheen's reflections in this book will make that happen.

Lift Up Your Heart

Not many people today have heard of *Lift Up Your Heart*, but this book has the power to bring miracles to the desperate and broken. I once met an amazing man who, after reading this book, overcame a life-long addiction to drugs and alcohol. Sheen speaks truth to power in this amazing guide to achieve spiritual peace. This book is like a spiritual sword one can take to the broken areas of one's life and ego. Sheen's reflections shine the light of Christ to transform and bring deliverance. In today's "me" culture, *Lift Up Your Heart* should be required reading.

Peace of Soul

In the opening chapter of this work, Sheen says, "There is no world peace unless there is soul peace." For those seeking the peace that surpasses all understanding, *Peace of Soul* is an off-the-beaten-path treasure that can lead souls toward God's peace in a noisy world. Peace on earth begins with you and me, and this book will help you break the chains of sin, anxiety, self-centeredness, unbelief, fear of death, and more.

Treasure in Clay

Treasure in Clay is a journey through the life of Fulton J. Sheen, from his boyhood in Peoria, to his public ministry in New York, to global missions to his work as a televangelist. Priests, seminarians, and people from all backgrounds are drawn to this work because it is an intimate snapshot of the life of one of the United States' most famous priests.

The World's First Love

Bishop Sheen's renowned portrait of the Blessed Virgin Mary will help you grow in your understanding of the Mother of God as well as of the dignity and beauty of women. Sheen emphasizes the need for the Mother of God and her role as Mediatrix. In this powerful Marian work, Sheen encourages us all to go to Jesus through Mary.

These Are the Sacraments

Do we fully understand the power of God in the seven Sacraments of the Church? Bishop Sheen's presentation of the Sacraments of the Catholic Church brings clear understanding of their power and application. This book will help you better understand the presence and the mystery of Christ in every stage of your sacramental life of faith.

Bibliography

Sheen, Fulton J. *These Are the Sacraments.* Hawthorn Books, 1962.

———. *Peace of Soul. Liguori,* Missouri: Liguori/Triumph, 1996.

———. *Three to Get Married.* New York: Scepter, 1996.

———. *The World's First Love.* San Francisco: Ignatius Press, 1996.

———. *Lift Up Your Heart.* Liguori, Missouri: Liguori/Triumph, 1997.

———. *Treasure in Clay:* The Autobiography of Fulton J. Sheen. New York: Image Books/Doubleday, 1980.

———. *Life of Christ.* New York: Image Books/Doubleday, 2008.

Notes

CHAPTER 1

1. A party line is one telephone circuit shared among two or more telephone service subscribers. —*Ed.*

2. See Luke 23:43.

CHAPTER 2

1. Theories vary widely regarding the unconscious; Sheen was working with the ideas of the time. —*Ed.*

CHAPTER 3

1. Sheen wrote with the conventions of his day, so he sometimes didn't use more general terms for men, women, etc. But he intends to include everybody. —*Ed.*

2. See Blaise Pascal, *Pensées*, no. 526.

3. See Romans 1:20.

CHAPTER 5

1. See Mark 15:30.

CHAPTER 7

1. Authorship of Hebrews is widely considered to be non-Pauline, even though some advocates for Pauline authorship can be found. —*Ed.*

CHAPTER 10

1. See the poem "Her Portrait" by Francis Thompson. —*Ed.*

CHAPTER 11

1. See John 15:19.

2. See Isaiah 6:3.

CHAPTER 12

1. Sheen is referring to the account of the woman who anoints the feet of Jesus, which appears in all four Gospels, though the details differ. The woman is unnamed except in John's Gospel, which calls her Mary of Bethany, who was often identified in tradition as Mary Magdalene. Most scholars today hold that they are different women. —*Ed.*

CHAPTER 14

1. See the poem "Desiderium Indesideratum" by Francis Thompson. —*Ed.*

CHAPTER 15

1. In human beings, knowledge starts with the senses but then the mind uses that sense data to formulate the ideas and concepts needed to understand things. The body and soul together are united in a substantial union to form the human person. —*Ed.*

2. Sheen is referring to a line in Augustine's *Confessions: Amor meus, pondus meum,* meaning "my love, my weight" (13.9.10). —*Ed.*

CHAPTER 16

1. Sheen is likely alluding to an excerpt from Saint Augustine's *Confessions*: "You have formed us for yourself, and our hearts are restless till they find rest in you." —*Ed.*

CHAPTER 18

1. See *Summa Theologica* by Thomas Aquinas, II–II, q. 35, art. 4, ad. 2.

2. See Luke 14:18.

CHAPTER 19

1. See Ecclesiastes 3:26.

CHAPTER 22

1. This should not be taken to mean that mental illness derives from some sin. Instead, Sheen is simply pointing out that at times an unrepented sin can cause distress to a person until they repent of the wrong they have done. —*Ed.*

CHAPTER 23

1. See Shakespeare's *Hamlet*, 3.I.83.

CHAPTER 25

1. See John 6:51.

2. Arcturus is one of the brightest stars in the night sky. Sheen is likely referring to Job 38:31, in which God describes his power over the stars. —*Ed.*

CHAPTER 26

1. In this passage, Sheen uses spellings which are now antiquated for the biblical books of Isaiah, Ezekiel, and Zechariah. —*Ed.*

CHAPTER 27

1. This thought is attributed to Nathan Hale, an American soldier executed by the British on September 22, 1776. —*Ed.*

2. See Revelations 5:10.

CHAPTER 28

1. See Matthew 26:40.

2. See 2 Corinthians 3:18.

3. See Luke 9:22.

4. See Luke 24:32.

CHAPTER 29

1. Sheen is referring to the Greek word *kosmos*. The word can be used to indicate the universe itself or all of humankind. —*Ed.*

2. See John 6:38.

Pauline
BOOKS & MEDIA

A mission of the Daughters of St. Paul

As apostles of Jesus Christ, evangelizing today's world:

We are CALLED to holiness
by God's living Word and Eucharist.

We COMMUNICATE the Gospel message
through our lives and through all
available forms of media.

We SERVE the Church
by responding to the hopes and needs
of all people with the Word of God,
in the spirit of St. Paul.

For more information visit our website:
www.pauline.org.

BOOKS & MEDIA

The Daughters of St. Paul operate book and media centers at the following addresses. Visit, call, or write the one nearest you today, or find us at www.paulinestore.org.

CALIFORNIA
3908 Sepulveda Blvd, Culver City, CA 90230 — 310-397-8676
3250 Middlefield Road, Menlo Park, CA 94025 — 650-369-4230

FLORIDA
145 S.W. 107th Avenue, Miami, FL 33174 — 305-559-6715

HAWAII
1143 Bishop Street, Honolulu, HI 96813 — 808-521-2731

ILLINOIS
172 North Michigan Avenue, Chicago, IL 60601 — 312-346-4228

LOUISIANA
4403 Veterans Memorial Blvd, Metairie, LA 70006 — 504-887-7631

MASSACHUSETTS
885 Providence Hwy, Dedham, MA 02026 — 781-326-5385

MISSOURI
9804 Watson Road, St. Louis, MO 63126 — 314-965-3512

NEW YORK
115 E. 29th Street, New York City, NY 10016 — 212-754-1110

SOUTH CAROLINA
243 King Street, Charleston, SC 29401 — 843-577-0175

TEXAS
No book center; for parish exhibits or outreach evangelization, contact: 210-569-0500, or SanAntonio@paulinemedia.com, or P.O. Box 761416, San Antonio, TX 78245

VIRGINIA
1025 King Street, Alexandria, VA 22314 — 703-549-3806

CANADA
3022 Dufferin Street, Toronto, ON M6B 3T5 — 416-781-9131

¡También somos su fuente para libros,
videos y música en español!